LITTLE STORIES, SIMPLE TRUTHS

THE JOY OF A PEANUTS CHRISTMAS

Reflections by Molly Wigand

CHRISTMAS MEANS
KNOWING WHAT MATTERS

Few contemporary holiday moments convey the meaning of Christmas better than Linus's part in the Christmas pageant put on by the Peanuts gang. He reflects the universal message of the season, and believers and nonbelievers alike can relate to his optimistic spirit and philosophical, yet uncomplicated faith.

Throughout the holiday comic strips, the Peanuts characters give voice to childlike goodness, optimism and generosity. Giving instead of receiving, putting aside our differences, and retelling the Biblical Christmas story—all these messages transcend nostalgia and hold up forever as emotional and authentic expressions of holiday goodness and love.

CHRISTMAS MEANS KNOWING WHAT MATTERS

CHRISTMAS MEANS KNOWING WHAT MATTERS

CHRISTMAS MEANS KNOWING WHAT MATTERS

CHRISTMAS MEANS KNOWING WHAT MATTERS

CHRISTMAS MEANS KNOWING WHAT MATTERS

CHRISTMAS MEANS KNOWING WHAT MATTERS

CHRISTMAS MEANS KNOWING WHAT MATTERS

CHRISTMAS MEANS KNOWING WHAT MATTERS

CHRISTMAS MEANS

FRIENDSHIP

At the heart of Charles Schulz's work (along with brilliantly evocative, minimalist drawings) is the friendship and camaraderie shared by his characters, the Peanuts gang. Whatever the situation, these lovable pals remain true to themselves. In her biography of her late husband, (who went by the nickname, "Sparky") Jean Schulz explained, "He could come up with ideas from almost any situation because his characters had such distinct personalities and idiosyncrasies."

From good old Charlie Brown to the perpetually crabby Lucy Van Pelt, the characters embody qualities that ring true for readers of all ages. Each member of the strip's cast represents a facet of human goodness. Charlie Brown stands for hope in the face of daunting odds. Linus is the innocent, reminding others what's important through his wise, sweet spirit. Schroeder is the temperamental artist, Sally the naïve free spirit. The group has its ups and downs, but through every story line the audience feels the undercurrent of loyalty and love.

At Christmastime, friendship means sending a card or having someone to skate with, but every day the strip celebrated the year round blessing of having friends.

CHRISTMAS MEANS FRIENDSHIP

CHRISTMAS MEANS FRIENDSHIP

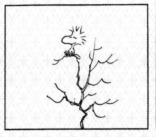

CHRISTMAS MEANS FRIENDSHIP

CHRISTMAS MEANS FRIENDSHIP

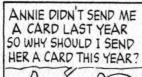

CHRISTMAS MEANS FRIENDSHIP

CHRISTMAS MEANS FRIENDSHIP

CHRISTMAS MEANS FRIENDSHIP

CHRISTMAS MEANS

GIFTS

The Peanuts gang accurately depicts children's attitudes toward gifts at the holidays. It's the season of giving, to be sure, but whether it's a dollar in Sally's greeting card or Lucy not getting her string of pearls from Schroeder, who among us doesn't focus on the getting, too? The honesty with which Sparky reveals his characters' attitudes and motivations resonates with readers of all ages. The Peanuts gang's childlike (and possibly flawed) understanding of the concept of giving is endearing in Sparky's hands.

We see both the best and worst of ourselves in these characters, and it's therapeutic to look into the mirror of childhood in order to accept the human frailties we share.

Sparky's drawings are priceless gifts to our culture, and with each rereading, they help us find and appreciate the goodness in the people we know and in the world outside our own.

CHRISTMAS MEANS GIFTS

CHRISTMAS MEANS GIFTS

I'M SENDING A CHRISTMAS CARD TO MICKEY MOUSE BECAUSE HE GAVE ME HIS SHOES..

Dear Mickey, Merry Christmas.

Thanks again for the shoes. Your friend, Spike

P.S. Just out of curiosity, why do you wear gloves all the time?

12-23

CHRISTMAS MEANS GIFTS

CHRISTMAS MEANS

BELIEVING

The Santa strips reveal that every one of the Peanuts gang is a true believer in Santa, and reading the children's letters helps reconnect adult readers with the magic of the Santa story.

The letters include the children's wish lists, but the correspondence goes far beyond those typical requests. From Sally's offer to help with Santa's mail to Linus's concern about the condition of the sleigh and reindeer, the Peanuts gang regards Santa as a person with needs and concerns. He's considered a friend who just happens to have the magical power to make Christmas dreams come true.

Sparky once said, "I would be satisfied if they wrote on my tombstone, 'He made people happy.'" Each of these Christmas comic strips has played a simple but undeniable part in making the artist's wish come true.

CHRISTMAS MEANS BELIEVING

CHRISTMAS MEANS BELIEVING

CHRISTMAS MEANS BELIEVING

CHRISTMAS MEANS BELIEVING

PEANUTS

WELL, DID YOU TELL SANTA CLAUS WHAT YOU WANT FOR CHRISTMAS?

Santa HERE TODAY

SURE.. I ALSO WISHED HIM A VERY HAPPY HANUKKAH...

12-23

WE DIDN'T HAVE MUCH TIME, BUT WE DISCUSSED JUDAS MACCABAEUS AND THE CLEANSING OF THE TEMPLE

IT'S NOT OFTEN THAT YOU FIND A SANTA CLAUS WHO'S INTERESTED IN RELIGION ...

SCHULZ

CHRISTMAS MEANS BELIEVING

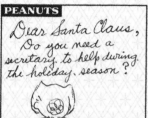

CHRISTMAS MEANS BELIEVING

CHRISTMAS MEANS
TRADITIONS

For 50 years (from 1950-2000), Sparky's iconic comic strip Peanuts has celebrated the gifts of friendship, childhood, and love. With these values at its heart, it's no wonder that the characters have become closely linked to the Christmas season. Sparky grew up in St. Paul, Minnesota. He was an avid hockey player who loved winter, an affinity that shows up in many of the holiday strips.

Sparky wove both the secular and religious components of Christmas into the characters' stories with fun, tenderness, and grace. Sharing the Peanuts characters' holiday fun has become a favorite tradition for many families over the years.

The Peanuts magic all started with the strips. And from Linus Van Pelt using his holiday stocking as a security blanket to young Sally Brown's impatience and hanging multiple stockings because hers are so small, Sparky's holiday comic strips reveal the heart and originality of each of his lovable characters and remind us what it's like to be a child at Christmas.

CHRISTMAS MEANS TRADITIONS

CHRISTMAS MEANS TRADITIONS

CHRISTMAS MEANS TRADITIONS

CHRISTMAS MEANS TRADITIONS

CHRISTMAS MEANS TRADITIONS

If you have enjoyed this book or it
has touched your life in some way,
we would love to hear from you.

Please send your comments to:
Hallmark Book Feedback
P.O. Box 419034
Mail Drop 100
Kansas City, MO 64141

Or e-mail us at:
booknotes@hallmark.com

PEANUTS.
by Schulz

SIGH

P ME, LINUS.. I
T TO MAKE A
IAL CHRISTMAS
D FOR THE LITTLE
-HAIRED GIRL..

DRAW A TREE, CHARLIE BROWN, WITH SOME TINY RED HEARTS HANGING ON IT..

THEN WRITE SOMETHING SORT OF PERSONAL AT THE BOTTOM...

WHAT'S GOING ON? IS MY SWEET BABBOO HELPING MY BIG BROTHER DRAW A CHRISTMAS CARD?

OKAY, YOU'RE ON!

I'M NOT YOUR SWEET BABBOO!!

THAT IS SO STUPID! THAT IS SO HUMONGOUSLY STUPID!

THERE! HOW DOES THAT LOOK? I DREW A TREE WITH LITTLE HEARTS ON IT..

"MERRY CHRISTMAS FROM YOUR SWEET BABBOO"?!

IT'S A FAMILY EXPRESSION..

".. AND JESSE BEGAT DA KING BEGAT SOLOMON WIFE OF URIAS; AND SOL ROBOAM BEGAT ABIA; AN

PEANUTS
featuring
"Good ol' Charlie Brown"
by SCHULZ

?IS MY SWEET
MY BIG BROTHER
AS CARD?

OKAY, YOU'RE ON!

"THE BOOK OF THE GENERATION OF JESUS CHRIST, THE SON OF DAVID, THE SON OF ABRAHAM"

"ABRAHAM BEGAT ISAAC; AND ISAAC BEGAT J AND JACOB BEGAT JUDAS AND HIS BRETHREN JUDAS BEGAT PHARES AND ZARA OF THAMAR; PHARES BEGAT ESROM; AND ESROM BEGAT ARA

'S A FAMILY
EXPRESSION..

"...AND JESSE BEGAT DAVID THE KING; AND DAVID THE KING BEGAT SOLOMON OF HER THAT HAD BEEN THE WIFE OF URIAS; AND SOLOMON BEGAT ROBOAM; AND ROBOAM BEGAT ABIA; AND ABIA BEGAT ASA..."

"...AND JACOB BEGAT JOSEPH THE HUSBAND OF MARY, OF WHOM WAS BORN JESUS, WHO IS CALLED CHRIST. SO ALL THE GENERATIONS FROM ABRAHAM TO DAVID ARE FOURTEEN GENERATIONS..."

"NOW THE BIRTH OF JESUS CHRIST WAS ON THIS WISE..."

WHY DIDN'T YOU JUST START WITH THE FIRST CHAPTER OF GENESIS WHILE YOU WERE AT IT?

DON'T
SARCA
"'TIS T
SEASO
BE JO